Connell Short Guide
to
J.D. Salinger's

———————

The Catcher
in the Rye

———————

by
Luke Neima

Contents

Introduction   1

A summary of the plot   2

Holden's voice   6

Catcher in the rye - the motif   18

"Comin Thro' The Rye" - the poem   24

Coming-of-age novel or teen fiction?   30

An author you could call up on the
telephone   37

NOTES

Five facts about The Catcher in the Rye   22
A short chronology   45
Further Reading   46

Introduction

At first glance, it's hard to understand why people are still outraged by *The Catcher in the Rye* – how is a novel written in 1951 still banned in some places, and barred from the school syllabus in many others?

Other than a bit of swearing, there's nothing all that outrageous about J.D. Salinger's first and only novel. Holden Caulfield, a lonely, angsty under-achiever, is expelled from yet another prep school, so he packs up his bags a couple of days before the Christmas holidays and leaves for a "madman" weekend in New York. He drinks scotch in piano bars, checks up on the ducks in Central Park, has a run-in with a prostitute, goes on a date, takes in a few movies and sneaks back home to visit his younger sister, Phoebe. Then he gets sick and is sent off to an unidentified institution.

Yet since its first publication in 1951 this short novel has been reprinted hundreds of times, sparked passionate debate and even been blamed for several murders. Why? What makes it so special?

Introducing a series of essays on the book, Harold Bloom asks: "Does *The Catcher in the Rye* promise to be of permanent eminence, or will it eventually be seen as an idealistic period-piece, which I think will be the fate of Harper Lee's *To Kill a Mockingbird* and Toni Morrison's *Beloved*, works as popular as Catcher continues to be?"

The novelist William Faulkner, says Bloom, "remarked that Holden's dilemma was his inability to find and accept an authentic mentor, a teacher or guide who could arouse his trust". It's a very American dilemma, and Holden "speaks for our scepticism, and for our need". Whether or not he will go on doing so in the years to come, however, is very much an open question.

A summary of the plot

Holden, aged 16, is either in a hospital or a mental institution. We don't know. But he has decided to tell us about the "madman" weekend in New York that led to him getting ill, and he starts with the Saturday before his boarding school, Pencey Prep, broke up for Christmas.

Holden has just been expelled – for the fourth time – and his favourite teacher, Mr Spencer, hedges his disappointment by justifying giving him a failing grade. Holden writes him off as a "phony" – he's the first of many adults Holden takes against during the book.

Later on that same evening Holden sees his conventional, good-looking room-mate, Ward Stradlater, return late from a date with Jane Gallagher, a girl Holden met two summers before. Holden is infuriated by Stradlater's casual attitude towards Jane; they have a fight; Holden ends up beaten up and bloody on the floor. He decides to sell his typewriter and make for New York City, even though he's supposed to be at school until Wednesday.

On the train Holden meets the mother of a boy he thinks of as "the biggest bastard" at the school, but he lies and says that he is popular, admired and respected. It's the first in a series of incidents that show how he can't resist making things up.

Once in New York, Holden heads for the Edmont Hotel. On the way, he asks the cab driver where the ducks in Central Park go during the winter, but doesn't get an answer. It's a question he'll keep asking throughout the book – and hints at the naivety, innocence and sense of wonder underlying all the destructive things he does.

Holden gets himself a room and watches the "perverts" in the opposite wing – a man cross-dressing and a couple squirting water out of their mouths at each other. Holden confesses that he's "probably the biggest sex maniac you ever saw", and decides to call up Faith Cavendish, a girl he's been told might be willing to sleep with him. She offers to meet Holden the next day but he panics and makes up an excuse to get out of it.

After flirting with three older women in the hotel bar, Holden takes a cab to Ernie's jazz club in Greenwich Village. There he runs into an ex-girlfriend of his older brother, who asks if he wants to join her and her date. Holden makes up another excuse and heads back to his hotel, resenting her for "ruining" his night.

But he's not sure what he wants. At his hotel, the elevator operator, Maurice, asks if he'd like to hire a prostitute for five dollars. Holden agrees. A young woman, Sunny, soon arrives at his door, but he can't bring himself to sleep with her. He pays her five dollars anyway, and asks if she'll agree to sit and talk instead.

She storms out and comes back with Maurice, who beats Holden up until he pays them an extra five dollars. After they leave, Holden is distraught – he even thinks about jumping out of the window, but decides against it.

The next day he meets two nuns at breakfast, and gives them ten dollars. After buying the record "Little Shirley Beans" for his little sister, he goes on a date with a girl named Sally Hayes. The two kiss on their way to the theatre, but Holden gets jealous when Sally starts talking to an old friend after the show. They go ice-skating at Radio City, where Sally asks if Holden will come over for Christmas Eve. He says he will, and asks Sally to run away with him to the country. She refuses, saying "we're both practically children" and tells Holden they both need to do some growing up first. Holden calls her a "pain in the ass".

After leaving the rink Holden arranges to see an old classmate, Carl Luce. They meet for a drink and Holden tries to get Luce to tell him about his sex life. Luce gets annoyed and leaves while

Holden gets drunk and calls Sally, saying he wants to see her on Christmas Eve, despite everything. Then he breaks down and wanders Central Park, trying to find the ducks, and accidentally shatters his little sister's record along the way.

He's cold and worries he'll die of pneumonia, which makes him think of his younger brother, Allie, who died of leukaemia. He sneaks home and finds that his parents are out – so he explains what's been going on to his little sister Phoebe. She's angry with him for hating everyone and everything, and asks him what he wants to do with himself. He says he'd like to be like "the catcher in the rye" from Robert Burns's poem, and stand out in a field of rye and catch children before they fall off the edge of a cliff.

Holden ends up visiting another teacher, Mr Antolini, who's offered him a place to stay. Mr Antolini gives Holden advice, and warns him that he's "riding for some kind of a terrible, terrible fall". Holden wakes later that night to find Mr Antolini stroking him on the head. Holden worries he's doing something "perverty", makes an excuse and leaves the apartment. He ends up sleeping on a bench at Grand Central Station. "It wasn't too nice," he says, "Don't ever try it. I mean it. It'll depress you."

He decides to strike out for the West, and leaves a note at his sister's school letting her know he's leaving and wants to see her one last time. When they meet, Holden's surprised to find that she's brought a suitcase and wants to go with him. The two fight and angrily walk through the park, but they make up when they reach the carousel. Holden buys her a ticket and watches her ride, and feels "so damn happy all of a sudden". He stands in the rain, crying, and his story comes to an end.

He says he doesn't want to get into how he went home and got "sick", but he does say he's getting ready for a new school in the fall. The novel ends with a little advice: "Don't ever tell anybody anything. If you do, you start missing everybody."

Holden's voice

The aspect of *The Catcher in the Rye* that critics praise above all else is its voice – the distinctive tone of its precocious, angst-ridden narrator, Holden Caulfield. A teenage narrator who swears freely and rants about whatever comes into his head was unheard of when the book was published in 1951. It is still rare now. The biographer and literary critic Ian Hamilton says that reading the novel taught him that "literature can speak for you, not just to you"; he is one of many who consider Holden Caulfield to be the voice of a generation.

J.D. Salinger immediately establishes how different his central character is to a typical narrator: Holden starts his story by telling us that he won't be following any of the literary conventions we might expect:

> *If you really want to hear about it, the first thing you'll probably want to know is where I was born, and what my lousy childhood was like, and how my parents were occupied and all before they had me, and all that David Copperfield kind of crap, but I don't feel like going into it, if you want to know the truth. In the first place that stuff bores me, and in the second place, my parents would have about two hemorrhages apiece if I told anything pretty personal about them.*

By having his narrator assert, right away, that his story will be very different from the "crap" written by canonical authors like Charles Dickens, Salinger shakes up our expectations. Holden maintains he's not making up a story – he's expressing something that's deeply personal and honest.

And it is the sincerity of Holden's voice that has swayed successive generations of readers. More persuasive than anything he says is the way he says it – Salinger not only mimics the slang and speech patterns of a young man from the 1950s, he also mimics the way Holden's thoughts move and the vocal tics he relies on.

Brian Way, a critic for the *New Left Review*, notes how Holden's voice balances "the blend of penetration and immaturity in judgment which is the mark of the intelligent adolescent" with the "school-boyish crudities of overstatement". The way Holden mixes flashes of insight with absurd, off-hand statements makes reading *The Catcher in the Rye* feel as if you're having a conversation with a real-life teenager – albeit one whose slang is a little dated.

The use of words like "crap" and "hell" add to this impression, and, while early reviews of *The Catcher in the Rye* were largely positive, some critics were taken aback by the "formidably excessive use of amateur swearing and coarse language", as Riley Hughes put it in Catholic World. For many readers at the time, it was shocking to read a book in which the narrator swore as frequently as Holden does – and there were worries that his voice would be a bad influence on younger readers.

It wasn't until 1955, four years after its publication, that anyone attempted to censor the book, but after that instances of censorship grew along with the book's popularity, particularly after it began to appear on school reading lists. Between 1966 and 1975 it was banned in schools more often than any other book in the United States, largely because of the coarse language it contains.[*]

[*] It continues to appear on the American Library Association's list of most frequently challenged books taught in school to this day - and was the sixth most challenged book in the United States as recently as 2009.

Holden's swearing, though, reflects his character – it's meant to show how angry he is, how different from the conventional, well-mannered young men he's surrounded by at prep school. From the way he dresses in a bright red hunting cap to the poverty of his language, he's very much an outsider, and he knows it.

Holden tells his readers he has "a lousy vocabulary", and, ironically, is as concerned with the way swearing influences children as his strongest censors. The word "fuck" appears six times in the novel, but Holden never uses it himself. Instead, he sees it scrawled on the walls of his little sister's school, and it infuriates him. He tells the reader:

It drove me damn near crazy. I thought how Phoebe and all the other little kids would see it, and how they'd wonder what the hell it meant... I kept wanting to kill whoever'd written it.

It's almost as if he's pre-empting his own critics.

Holden's cursing is a means of emphasising his alienation from mainstream society, and is only one small aspect of Salinger's extensive reproduction of the slang of the day. The vocabulary in the book ranges from Holden's favourite adjectives – "Goddam," "phony" and "lousy" – to descriptions of people doing "everything backasswards", the values of Pencey

Prep being "strictly for the birds" and anything and everything being punctuated with an "and all".

David Lodge, writing in the *New York Times*, has praised Salinger's reproduction of the vocabulary of his day, saying that there is something magical and musical about it. He describes the elegance of Holden's voice with the Russians literary term skaz*: "a nice word with echoes of jazz and scat in it, which uses the repetitions and redundancies of ordinary speech to produce an effect of sincerity and authenticity — and humor". The way Holden repeats himself, contradicts himself and occasionally runs on and on allows Salinger to expose in detail the way his character's mind works – and make him feel authentic and true to life.

In a letter he wrote in 1957, Salinger acknowledged that the importance of the first person viewpoint in *The Catcher in the Rye* meant there could never be a movie of the novel:

> For me, the weight of the book is in the narrator's voice, the non-stop peculiarities of it, his personal, extremely discriminating attitude to his reader-listener, his asides about gasoline rainbows in street puddles, his philosophy or way

* The word is used for any narrative that is defined by its emphasis on oral speech - especially those that use dialect and slang to create a particular character. John Mullan uses it to describe *Catcher* as well as Martin Amis's *Money* and DBC Pierre's *Vernon God Little*.

of looking at cowhide suitcases and empty toothpaste cartons – in a word, his thoughts. He can't legitimately be separated from the first-person technique.

The Catcher in the Rye, Salinger suggests, isn't about events that can be filmed. It's about the thoughts and character of one teenage boy – something that could never be reproduced in a movie theatre.

It took Salinger a long time to find the right way of telling his tale, however. Ten years before *The Catcher in the Rye* was published, he sold "Slight Rebellion Off Madison" to the *New Yorker.* The story would become chapter 17 of the finished novel, but one dramatic difference makes it nearly unrecognisable – it's in the third person.

The short story revolves around the argument between Holden and Sally after they go skating at Radio City:

> *"You don't see what I mean at all."*
> *"Maybe I don't. Maybe you don't either," Sally said.*
> *Holden stood up with his skates slung over one shoulder.*
> *"You give me a royal pain," he announced quite dispassionately.*

Immediately, one notices how muted the words feel without Holden's voice guiding us to what matters in the conversation. Phrases like "he announced quite dispassionately" underscore the gulf between the third- person narrator – whose vocabulary is more technical and assured than Holden's would ever be – and Holden himself. When Salinger puts the scene in the first person, however, he transforms it:

> *"You don't see what I mean at all."*
> *"Maybe I don't. Maybe you don't either," old Sally said. We both hated each other's guts by that time. You could see there wasn't any sense in trying to have an intelligent conversation. I was sorry as hell I'd started it. "C'mon, let's get outa here," I said. "You give me a royal pain in the ass, if you want to know the truth."*
> *Boy, did she hit the ceiling when I said that. I know I shouldn't've said it and I probably wouldn't've ordinarily, but she was depressing the hell out of me.*

The first person voice allows the reader direct access to Holden's thoughts and feelings – and it helps the reader identify with him. The critic Eberhard Alsen argues that Salinger decided to use the first person in order to create a contrast between Holden's "blind spots" and his occasional flashes of objectivity. In this scene, for example, Holden knows that he shouldn't have been so rude to Sally, but what he doesn't realise is how much

Sally's refusal to live in the woods with him has upset him. The reader knows Sally is right – Holden's idea is impractical, even crazy – but Holden doesn't. What he refuses to face is the realities of the world, and the fact that he's still, in many ways, a child. The mature reader can read between the lines and understand this.

These "blind spots" are one of the reasons why Holden's voice feels so real. The things he notices or mentions depend on his moods – and he is moody. He swings between moments of immaturity, selfishness, anger and honesty, and these emotional changes all affect his judgement. Because Holden contradicts himself so often, and misses so many important emotional truths, he is what is known in literary terms as an unreliable narrator. Up to a point, of course, he's aware of this, announcing in the third chapter:

I'm the most terrific liar you ever saw in your life. It's awful. If I'm on my way to the store to buy a magazine, even, and somebody asks me where I'm going, I'm liable to say I'm going to the opera. It's terrible.

And yet, even though Holden admits he is a liar, and continues to lie throughout the book, he still manages to convince his readers he is being honest with them. This is, in part, due to the reasons for his lies – reasons of which he isn't always entirely conscious.

The first lie Holden tells is to his history teacher, Mr Spencer. He says he has to get some equipment from the gym, which he explains to the reader is "a sheer lie" and "terrible" behaviour. But immediately before Holden tells the lie he explains that he pities Mr Spencer and can't stand to stay with him: "I felt sorry as hell for him, all of a sudden. But I just couldn't hang around there any longer." Some part of Holden knows that telling the truth – that he can't stand Mr Spencer's "sad old bathrobe" and "grippy smell of Vicks Nose Drops" – would be far more hurtful than telling a white lie.

A similar incident occurs on the train to New York, when Holden tries to convince Mrs Morrow that her son is a good person. He feels "sort of sorry" about lying, but again his lies are excusable. Holden explains:

I'll bet, after all the crap I shot, Mrs Morrow'll keep thinking of him now as this very shy, modest guy that wouldn't let us nominate him for president.

The reader can tell that Holden is not necessarily telling lies because he is "terrible" – instead, it seems far more likely that he is lying because he is sympathetic and wants Mrs Morrow to feel good about herself and her son.

As well as enabling us to see that Holden's

motives for lying are often good ones, Salinger uses another narrative trick to make his hero seem engaging. He himself alludes to it in his letter, when he refers to Holden's "personal, extremely discriminating attitude to his reader-listener". Other than Phoebe, Holden feels alienated from everyone he meets: he has no one to whom he can tell his troubles. But when he writes about his experiences he finds someone: you, the reader. The relationship between narrator and reader is carefully developed, with everything in the novel directed firmly to "you".

The story opens with the words, "If you really wanna hear about it..." It is as if we are already in the middle of a conversation with Holden – and the slight defensiveness in his tone makes it seem as if we've put him on the spot by asking him to tell his story. And in a way we have: after all we've made the effort to open the front cover. We've made the first move.

It doesn't take long before we get the feeling that Holden has started to like us as his readers. When he describes his brother, Allie, he says: "You'd like him" – aligning the reader with his point of view in stark contrast to the Ackleys and Stradlaters and other phonies of the world.

The reader becomes an insider, a companion who always shares Holden's critical insight. At Ernie's piano bar, for instance, Holden says: "You should've heard the crowd... You would've puked."

And when he writes about his little sister, Phoebe, he says "You'd like her" twice, as if the reader's good judgment is the best way of making his point. The tone of the book is that of a confession to an old friend – and treating a reader like an old friend can be a very effective way to win his or her sympathy.

Some critics argue that Salinger goes too far with all this, and that his use of Holden's voice is manipulative, or, in Jonathan Yardley's phrase, an "easy exploitation of the reader's emotion". Yardley writes:

> Give your protagonist a dead younger brother and a cute little sister... and the rest is strictly downhill. From first page to last, "The Catcher in the Rye" is an exercise in button-pushing, and the biggest button it pushes is the adolescent's uncertainty and insecurity.

By mimicking the uncertainty and insecurity almost all adolescents experience, Holden Caulfield draws young readers to him because he often seems to be putting their own experiences into words. Yardley's objection to this technique is that Holden doesn't do much with it after drawing them in: he continues to rant and rave, never finds a way of making himself feel better, and may simply lead impressionable readers to indulge in "self-pity" and "resentment" towards grown-ups and society.

In 2014's Connell Guides Essay Prize, the

winner, Susanna Crawford, writes about exactly this experience. On first reading *The Catcher in the Rye,* she sympathised with Holden and thought of him as a "role model". Returning to the book when a little older, however, she found Holden's angst too much:

> Any sane human would realise that there are people starving to death in the same city where Holden is wasting his parents' cash on alcohol and prostitutes. In short, *The Catcher in the Rye* has made a bigger impact on my life than anything else because it has shown me exactly how not to act.

Coming to terms with Holden's weaknesses and his blind spots – and understanding his true unreliability as a narrator – can engender a sense of betrayal, especially in younger readers who initially value his honesty. Older readers, on the other hand, may sense from the first that there's something wrong with Holden's voice, and that his story isn't the only one being told in the book.

Catcher in the rye - the motif

We know from Holden's voice that he's sensitive, angry, and unreliable, but why is he like that? Critics have advanced all sorts of theories – from a disillusionment with capitalism to Oedipal desires to a slowly-awakening Zen spiritualism – and though all these may have their merits, a good place to start is with the book's central motif: "the catcher in the rye". Holden says being "catcher in the rye" is the only thing that could make him happy, and Salinger makes it the title of the book – two fairly large clues that the symbol is worth a closer look.

The first time the image appears is while Holden is wandering through Central Park, depressed and alone. He hears a child singing "If a body catch a body coming through the rye", and it cheers him up. He admires how the child is "singing for the hell of it", unaware of the people around him and the cars zooming by, content and happy in the simplicity of childhood.

The phrase sits at the back of his mind, and when his little sister asks him what he wants to do with his life, he enlarges on it, telling her he wants to "be the catcher in the rye:"

I'm standing on the edge of some crazy cliff. What I

*have to do, I have to catch everybody if they start to
go over the cliff – I mean if they're running and they
don't look where they're going I have to come out
from somewhere and catch them. That's all I'd do
all day. I'd just be the catcher in the rye and all. I
know it's crazy, but that's the only thing I'd really
like to be.*

Holden's description of saving children from
falling over a cliff is certainly odd – maybe even a
bit crazy – but as a symbol it's simple and effective.*
Holden idealises the innocence of childhood and
wants to preserve and protect it – his own as much
as everyone else's.

Why does Holden feel the need to save
children? First and foremost, children are the only
people who aren't "phony" in Holden's mind.
Children like Phoebe, or the girl whose skates he
laces up in the park, or the two boys he meets in
the Natural History Museum, are the only
characters he ever qualifies as "nice". To Holden,
childhood is an oasis of purity in a corrupt adult
world. It's understandable that he wishes children
would stay pure forever, innocent and far from the
"cliff" that leads to the artificiality and phoniness

* The "catcher in the rye" symbol is closely linked to the falling
metaphor embedded throughout the novel. The "fall" Mr
Antolini warns Holden about and the "feeling" that he'll "just go
down, down, down" as he steps off curbs on his last day in the
city both relate to Holden's conception of himself as catcher in
the rye, "standing on the edge of some crazy cliff."

of adulthood.

The central theme of Salinger's work, say the critics Arthur Heiserman and James E. Miller Jr, is stated explicitly in one of his short stories: "For Esmé – with Love and Squalor". In the story Salinger quotes a passage from Dostoevsky: "Fathers and teachers, I ponder 'What is hell?' I maintain that it is the suffering of being unable to love." This is Salinger's diagnosis of the world, too, say Heiserman and Miller: "if we cannot love, we cannot live".

The themes of childhood and the loss of innocence have long been central preoccupations of Western literature. In Salinger's work these themes are almost an obsession: his heroes are constantly attempting to return to a lost Eden.

Salinger's childism is consubstantial with his concern for love and neurosis. Adultism is precisely "the suffering of being unable to love", and it is that which produces neurosis. Everyone able to love in Salinger's stories is either a child or a man influenced by a child. All the adults not informed by love and innocence are by definition phonies and prostitutes. "You take adults, they always look lousy when they're asleep with their mouths open, but kids don't... They look all right." Kids like Phoebe shut up when they haven't anything to say. They even say 'thank you' when you tighten their skates, and they don't go behind a post to button their pants.

In *The Catcher in the Rye,* the character

struggling most with the transition from innocence to phoniness is Holden. Though he idealises purity and criticises the artificiality of the adult world, he's growing up and it's made him as "phony" as everyone else. He's an admitted liar, he continually makes up excuses to get out of doing things he doesn't want to do and he can't help letting his family and friends down. The person who most needs catching from a fall is Holden himself.

Holden's desire to save children, however, is heightened by memories of his little brother, Allie – an innocent child who died and whom Holden could do nothing to protect. He idealises Allie, describes him as if he were still alive, speaks to him when he feels depressed and even writes Stradlater's composition letter about the way his brother covered his baseball glove with poems in "green ink". Holden describes how he felt the night Allie died:

> *I broke all the goddam windows with my fist, just for the hell of it. I even tried to break all the windows on the station wagon we had that summer, but my hand was already broken and everything by that time, and I couldn't do it.*

Holden is still angry, and his anger is a way of channelling his grief for a brother still very alive in his mind. Being a "catcher in the rye" is, in part, a fantasy about saving the person he thinks of as "a

FIVE FACTS ABOUT
THE CATCHER IN THE RYE

1.

Since its first publication, more than 65 million copies of *The Catcher in the Rye* have been sold. Around 250,000 copies of the book are sold each year - about 685 per day.

2.

In the novel, Holden Caufield is described as looking like Harvey in the 1937 film *Captains Courageous*, played by Freddie Bartholomew (right).

3.

Holden uses the word "phony" 35 times in the book. He also says "crazy" 77 times and "goddam" 245 times.

4.

Mark David Chapman – the man who shot John Lennon – was reading a copy of *The Catcher in the Rye* when he was arrested.

5.

According to a recent biogrpahy, Salinger's pick-up line was "I'm J.D. Salinger and I wrote *The Catcher in the Rye*".

Opposite: Freddie Bartholomew in Captains Courageous *(1937)*

thousand times nicer than the people you know that're alive and all".

Janet Malcolm points out that Holden's rescue fantasy is also deeply influenced by the constant stream of negative experiences he has in the adult world. Adults continually disappoint him – from his brother DB, who sells out and moves to Hollywood; to his teachers Mr Spencer and Mr Antolini, who seem more concerned with themselves than Holden; from the prostitute Sally and her pimp Sunny, who cheat him out of five dollars; to his own parents, who ship him off to boarding school when his brother dies. Holden simply cannot find adults who he can communicate with and trust. This is part of the reason why he dreams of being the saviour of innocence, and it's also the reason why Phoebe is the only person he'll let pull him away from his own self- destructive desires.

"Comin Thro' The Rye" – the poem

The catcher in the rye metaphor is intricate and well- developed, and another way into the many things it stands for is an analysis of the Robert Burns poem that inspired it:

O, Jenny's a' weet, poor body,
Jenny's seldom dry;
She draigl't a' her petticoattie
Comin thro' the rye.
Comin thro the rye, poor body,
Comin thro' the rye,
She draigl't a'her petticoatie,
Comin thro the rye!
Gin a body meet a body
Comin thro' the rye,
Gin a body kiss a body,
Need a body cry?
Comin thro the rye, poor body,
Comin thro' the rye,
She draigl't a'her petticoatie,
Comin thro' the rye!
Gin a body meet a body
Comin thro' the glen,
Gin a body kiss a body,
Need the warld ken?
Comin thro the rye, poor body,
Comin thro' the rye,
She draigl't a'her petticoatie,
Comin thro' the rye

(Modern English translation)
Oh, Jenny's all wet, poor body,
Jenny's seldom dry;
She's draggin' all her petticoats
Comin' through the rye.

Comin' through the rye, poor body,
Comin' through the rye.
She's draggin' all her petticoats
Comin' through the rye.
Should a body meet a body
Comin' through the rye,
Should a body kiss a body,
Need anybody cry?
Comin' through the rye, poor body,
Comin' through the rye.
She's draggin' all her petticoats
Comin' through the rye.
Should a body meet a body
Comin' through the glen,
Should a body kiss a body,
Need all the world know, then?
Comin' through the rye, poor body,
Comin' through the rye.
She's draggin' all her petticoats
Comin' through the rye.

Burns's poem asks two major questions, both of which are constantly on Holden's mind: is casual sex acceptable ("Gin a body kiss a body")? And can people live outside the norms of society ("Need the warld ken")? For Burns, the questions are connected, and his poem laments the way society strips all naturalness out of human interaction.

The same is true in Salinger's work. Sex is a difficult topic for Holden because he can't come to terms with how to love others in a society where he doesn't have a place. "Sex is something I just don't understand," he says. "I swear to God I don't." He never knows what's expected of him: what's right and what's wrong when interacting with women.

The main object of Holden's desire and love throughout the book is Jane Gallagher, "the girl next door" whom he can't stop thinking about and never manages to talk to on the telephone. Carl F. Strauch interprets Holden's obsession with Jane's checkers style – she always keeps her kings in the back row – as a metaphor for Holden's own frustrated sexual desires. Keeping kings at the back of the board symbolises "the impotence of Holden's secret world, for the kings should range freely over the checkerboard".

Holden's approach to sexuality is remarkably similar to Jane's approach to checkers: he likes the idea of sex but never acts on it. He continually puts off phoning Jane, and when he has the chance to see her he decides he's "not in the mood". His other sexual efforts are just as restrained: when he calls up Faith Cavendish to make a date, he invents an excuse to get out of seeing her the next day; and when Sunny, the prostitute, comes to his room he pretends he is recovering from surgery on his "spinal canal" and asks her to just sit and talk to him instead.

Unlike the other young men he knows, Holden feels inhibited by sympathy in his dealings with women. When it comes to sex, he says, his problem is "I stop. Most guys don't. I can't help it." Holden respects a woman's request to stop, and his refusal to go along with what society – and other men – suggest he should do is, perhaps, a sign of nobility in his character.

When he's with Sunny, for example, he can't stop himself thinking of her as a person rather than simply as a sex object. She asks if she can hang up her dress and he says: "I thought of her going in a store and buying it, and nobody in the store knowing she was a prostitute and all... It made me feel sad as hell — I don't know why exactly." Though Holden may not understand, the reader knows he's too sensitive and idealistic to pay for sleeping with a girl he can't help seeing as a normal person with an internal life of her own.

What Holden wants in a relationship is more akin to what Carl Luce describes as "both a physical and a spiritual experience". Though Holden calls himself a "sort of an atheist", there is a deep element of spiritual significance running through his understanding of the world – most obvious when he speaks out loud to his dead brother, Allie, but also clear when he tries to pray and fails. Though he says "I like Jesus and all", he's distracted by thoughts of the disciples and the way they "keep letting Him down". The Church, like all other institutions, feels corrupt to Holden – love, spiritual or physical, is something he keeps hoping and failing to find amid the "phoniness" of the mainstream adult world.

When Holden asks his friend Ackley "what's the routine on joining a monastery?" he is serious; he is actually "toying with the idea of joining one". He repeats this dream in another form when he asks Sally to run away to a cabin in the woods with him. Like Burns's narrator, Holden wants to know whether or not he can find a way of living outside society while maintaining the human relationships that mean something to him. Will he have to do it alone? Or is there someone else who can go with him – another innocent, like Phoebe?

Although Salinger's novel draws strongly on the central idea of Burns's poem, there is a crucial difference. "Comin Thro' the Rye" is all about movement – about a journey being taken – while Holden's interpretation emphasises staying in one place, on the verge of a cliff, and waiting. His dreams of moving to a monastery or a cabin in the woods underline his feeling that it's not him who needs to change, but society itself.

The way Holden describes the Museum of Natural History perfectly summarises the static comfort and safety he longs for – a simple version of the world in which everything always stays the same:

The best thing, though, in that museum was that everything always stayed right where it was.

*Nobody'd move. You could go there a hundred
thousand times, and that Eskimo would still be just
finished catching those two fish, the birds would still
be on their way south, the deers would still be
drinking out of that water hole, with their pretty
antlers and their pretty, skinny legs, and that squaw
with the naked bosom would still be weaving that
same blanket. Nobody'd be different. The only thing
that would be different would be you.*

Holden's refusal to move forward in life, to grow up
and to finish mourning for Allie are all
encapsulated in the novel's central motif – his
dream of becoming a "catcher in the rye".

Coming-of-age novel or teen fiction?

Adam Gopnick, writing in the *New Yorker* shortly
after Salinger's death in 2010, says that "in
American writing, there are three perfect books
which seem to speak to every reader and condition:
Huckleberry Finn, *The Great Gatsby*, and *The
Catcher in the Rye*. Of the three, only *Catcher*
defines an entire region of human experience: it is
– in French and Dutch as much as in English – the
handbook of the adolescent heart." Gopnick is not
alone in describing *The Catcher in the Rye* as one

of the most important American bildungsromans[*] –
a literary term for a coming-of-age story where the
protagonist undergoes the psychological and
moral growth associated with the passage from
youth to adulthood. Since the Enlightenment,
Western literature has returned again and again to
themes of childhood and the loss of innocence. *The
Catcher in the Rye* is in a long tradition that runs
from Rousseau's *Emile* through Voltaire's *Candide*,
on through the young Wordsworth's *Lines Written
A Few Miles Above Tintern Abbey* to Mark Twain's
Huckleberry Finn.

But even though the novel fits perfectly into this
tradition of growth and self-discovery, it has more
recently been drawn into one of publishing's most
lucrative genres: teen fiction. You'll now see copies
of Salinger's book gracing the shelves of bookshops
alongside *Harry Potter* and *The Hunger Games*.
Though these novels are also about growing up and
deal with psychological development, you'd be
hard pressed to find a literary critic willing to
describe them with any German words, let alone
sit them alongside the hallowed classics of the
Western canon.

* In German, bildung means education and roman story, so a
"bildungsroman" is literally an "education-story". One of the
first major bildungsromans was Goethe's *Wilhelm Meister's
Apprenticeship*, and the genre includes novels like Charles
Dickens's *Great Expecations,* Somerset Maugham's *Of Human
Bondage* and James Joyce's *A Portrait of the Artist as a Young
Man.*

So where does *The Catcher in the Rye* really fit? This question was at the heart of the first significant critical attack on the book, George Steiner's 1959 essay, 'The Salinger Industry'. Steiner claims that Salinger's work lacks any real literary merit and merely "flatters the very ignorance and moral shallowness of his young readers". Novelist Norman Mailer was just as damning in a scathing critique he made the same year: "Salinger is everyone's favourite. I seem to be alone in finding him no more than the greatest mind ever to stay in prep school." For both Steiner and Mailer, and other critics who followed their lead, *The Catcher in the Rye* is nothing more than an accomplished teen novel.

Its most important literary forbear, of course, is Mark Twain's *The Adventures of Huckleberry Finn.* Twain's book, like Salinger's, uses the first-person voice of a teenager, incorporates slang, develops a conflict between the young man and adult society and is organised around the character of the narrator rather than events in the book itself. The acerbic Jewish-American critic Leslie Fiedler, however, argues that Salinger's work falls short of the standard set by Twain. Writing about what he calls "the Good Bad Boy" in American literature, Fiedler says that Salinger and the "beat" writer Jack Kerouac "attempt to project images of their own lost youth in the guise of Huckleberry Finn". Yearning still for boyhood, they "speak in their books through the boy's mask in a language as far removed from literate adult speech as was Huck's. Their prep-school or hipsterish sublanguages fail, however, to become the kind of poetry which Twain succeeded in making".

What being a young person meant in the 1950s was drastically different than what it meant in the 1880s, when Twain was writing. And what does set *The Catcher in the Rye* apart from other bildungsromans – as well as from other works of teen fiction – is that it was published at the moment that an entirely new social group was emerging around the world: the teenager.

Salinger specialist Dr. Sarah Graham, in an interview with the BBC, observed that before the 1950s people went through their teenage years with no sense of having a particular kind of separate identity. But by the fifties things had changed. Teenagers were all in high school for the first time, there wasn't the looming threat of war to force them into early responsibility, and the post-war economic boom meant not only that they didn't have to work but also that they had generous allowances to spend – on goods and culture increasingly tailored for them. They had time to think – and to think differently from their parents' generation – and Holden Caulfield became the poster child of this new way of life.

Sarah Graham goes further, arguing that reading *The Catcher in the Rye* actually helped to produce the feelings of existential angst that are now so commonly associated with being a teenager. Louis Menand agrees, writing in the *New Yorker*:

> The whole emotional burden of adolescence is that you don't know why you feel unhappy, or angry, or out of it. The appeal of *The Catcher in the Rye*, what makes it addictive, is that it provides you with a reason. It gives a content to chemistry.

Holden can provide a very simple, persuasive message to disaffected teenagers: the reason you feel unhappy is that society is phony and the best way to react is to refuse to be a part of it. Holden rebels in the only way he knows how: playing truant, drinking, swearing and wearing clothes that make him stick out – it's not hard to see the body piercings and hair dyes of later generations in the bright red hunting cap that shocks his preppy classmates at Pencey.

Another reason Holden works so well as a representative of the teenage experience is how easy it is to relate to him. Holden Caulfield isn't just a teenager. He's an archetype of the whole teenage experience.

The power of the Holden archetype is evident in the influence he has had over succeeding generations. The American film critic Raymond

Haberski even argues that "most young male characters in the movies are based on the character of Holden Caulfield [because] every young man goes through the experiences of Holden Caulfield". Haberski groups together movies as diverse as *The Graduate, Diner, Dead Poets Society, Rushmore, American Beauty* and *The Royal Tenenbaums* as all being informed by the model provided in Salinger's book.

Its influence is just as apparent in literature as in film. Gerald Rosen analyses the book as "the prescient portrait of an attempt to create a counterculture" – and argues that it was the foundation for the tradition of outsider-narratives that would come to define American literature from the Beat* generation onwards.

The Catcher in the Rye's role as a reference point for American counter-culture helps to explain why the book, only a modest success when first released, soon became a cultural phenomenon. Cultural critic Morris Dickstein notes that it "didn't become a cult book until the ensuing decade, when the much larger youth culture kicked in". For Dickstein, Holden's story

---

* The Beat writers were a loosely grouped collection of authors writing in the later 1950s, including Jack Kerouac, Allen Ginsberg and William Burroughs. They were united by their thematic exploration of subcultures of drug addiction, sexual freedom and drifting, as well as through their stylistic emphasis on free self-expression and their anti-establishment, anti-political values.

became popular because it was a new creature created for a new generation – not a bildungsroman but an anti-bildungsroman: "*The Catcher in the Rye* is not a growing-up novel but a not-growing-up novel." Unlike the protagonists in previous bildungsromans, Holden never does find his place in society, and nor does he want to.

This may be why the book has gone on speaking to successive generations. Now more than ever, maintaining a youthful lifestyle well into chronological "adulthood" is glamourised by popular media. Dickstein compares Holden's determinedly youthful existence to characters in the most popular sitcoms over the last 25 years:

> *Seinfeld, Sex and the City*, Lena Dunham's *Girls*, all of them [are] Peter Pannish fantasies of not settling down, hanging loose, hooking up, experimenting with one's identity, playing the field forever.

To Leslie Fiedler, however, *The Catcher in the Rye* is symptomatic of what he sees as the weakness of the American novel in general: its preoccupation with children, and in particular boys, and its tendency to avoid adult passion. In a provocative essay in 1948, Fiedler ascribed this weakness to

> the regressiveness of American life, its implacable nostalgia for the infantile, at once

wrongheaded and somehow admirable. The mythic America is boyhood – and who would dare to be startled to realise that two (and the two most popular, the two most absorbed, I think) of the handful of great books in our native heritage are customarily to be found, illustrated, on the shelves of the Children's Library.

He is talking about *Moby Dick* and *Huckleberry Finn*, of course. *The Catcher in the Rye* had not been written when Fielder published his essay, though it had by the time he developed it into a book, *Love and Death in the American Novel*, 20 years later. And in this he includes Salinger in the tradition he deplores.

An author you could call up on the telephone

At one point in *The Catcher in the Rye*, Holden describes his ideal reading experience:

> *What really knocks me out is a book that, when you're all done reading it, you wish the author that wrote it was a terrific friend of yours and you could call him up on the phone whenever you felt like it.*

J.D. Salinger was not, as many fans learned to their bitter disappointment, an author you could call up on the telephone. Two years after publishing *The Catcher in the Rye* he moved to a private estate in Cornish, New Hampshire, where he quickly acquired a reputation for refusing to grant interviews, respond to fan mail or speak to just about anyone other than his close family and friends.

Yet though Salinger is nothing like the author Holden describes in the passage above, he is remarkably like Holden. His retreat to the woods parallels the one Holden suggests to Sally, and his rejection of the media and the phoniness of celebrity would have undoubtedly been approved of by his most famous character.

Over the years many critics have examined the links between Salinger's youth and Holden's, and there is good reason to do so. A friend of Salinger's, Shirley Blaney, once asked him if his book was autobiographical, and he said: "Sort of. My boyhood was very much the same as that of the boy in the book, and it was a great relief telling people about it." Writing about Holden was an act of catharsis* for Salinger – and the relief he felt is often experienced by his readers as well.

Salinger endured the same kind of prep school

* The earliest literary critic, Aristotle, was puzzled by the fact that tragic plays left audiences relieved and exalted rather than depressed. He came up with the idea of tragedy as "katharsis" or "purification". Witnessing tragic acts, he argued, purged away excess emotions of fear and pity, leaving the passions balanced and healthy.

Opposite: J.D. Salinger

education that Holden suffers through – and was even sent away to military academy, a fate Holden is threatened with by his father. In Ian Hamilton's biography of Salinger, In *Search of J. D. Salinger*, an old classmate paints a portrait of the young Jerome – a rebellious student who doesn't quite fit in:

> Both of us hated the military regime and often wondered why we didn't leave the school. He enjoyed breaking the rules, and several times we both slipped off the academy grounds at 4 A.M. to enjoy a breakfast in the local diner. It was a great surprise to me that he returned to school for a second year.

Like Holden, Salinger skipped class and broke the rules. He was also, like Holden, a talker, an exhibitionist and an outsider. Another classmate remembers:

> He loved conversation... He liked people, but he couldn't stand stuffed shirts. Jerry was aware that he was miscast in the military role. He was all legs and angles, very slender... He always stuck out like a sore thumb in a long line of cadets.

When Salinger writes about how alienating institutions can be, and how bleak it feels not to fit in, his writing feels so honest and sincere because it reflects his own experience. But the way he portrayed his youth changed drastically as he grew older. Warren French shows how the different versions of Holden Caulfield evolved from a young man defeated by the world and aware of his own shortcomings – as in the story, "I'm Crazy" – into a portrait of an inveterate outsider, desperately seeking an escape route from contemporary society. Holden went from an average teenager to a character sharing some of the characteristics of a tragic hero.

Why did Salinger's ideas change? A critical reading gaining ground in recent years points to the influence of his experiences in World War II. We know that Salinger took the working draft of *The Catcher in the Rye* with him to the beaches of Normandy, and that he worked on his novel as he crossed the streets of newly liberated Paris and kept at it even after liberating a concentration camp from the Germans. Salinger's daughter, Margaret Ann Salinger, says her father's experience of the concentration camp stayed with him forever. He told her: "You never really get the smell of burning flesh out of your nose entirely, no matter how long you live."

His daughter's testimony reinforces the idea that the horrors of war changed the way Salinger thought about things. Kenneth Slawenski argues that the experience gave his writing a depth and maturity it had previously lacked. The selfishness and confusion apparent in early drafts of the novel gives way to something "noble" – and the sense that Holden's anguish relates to universal truths. Holden's struggle, Slawenski suggests, echoes the spiritual journey of the author himself:

> In both author and character, the tragedy is the same: a shattered innocence. Holden's reaction is shown through his scorn of adult phoniness and compromise. Salinger's reaction was personal despondency, through which his eyes were opened to the darker forces of human nature.

Salinger may have once thought his old school friends were phonies, just as Holden does, but they too would have had to face up to the grim reality of the war. Salinger may well have been thinking of dead soldiers when he wrote the final line of his novel: "Don't ever tell anybody anything. If you do, you start missing everybody."

Although it is tempting to understand Holden's grief and angst as a direct expression of Salinger's wartime experiences there are, of course, large gaps between Salinger and the character of Holden Caulfield. Ron Rosenbaum notes the reasons why we shouldn't assume the two are the same, not least because of the variety of characters who contradict Holden and try to teach him about himself.

Holden's idealised younger sister, Phoebe, for instance, rejects Holden's angst in a way that even he has grudgingly to respect. Salinger's own understanding of the world – and of Holden – also ring out in the words of Mr Antolini, who warns Holden against self-destruction. Mr Antolini, Rosenbaum tells us, isn't giving the kind of advice a phony adult would. He's being perceptive and sympathetic and understands all too well what's wrong with Holden's "simplistic black-and-white hate-the-phonies attitude". He could almost be an older, more-experienced Holden passing on advice to a kindred spirit.

The clearest cipher for Salinger in the novel is Holden's older brother D.B. Not only does D.B. go by his first two initials, he's an author who wrote a "terrific book of short stories" – one of which, The Secret Goldfish, sounds remarkably similar to Salinger's "A Perfect Day for Bananafish". Holden tells his reader: "my brother D.B. was in the Army for four goddam years. He was in the war, too – he landed on D-Day and all – but I really think he hated the Army worse than the war." D.B.'s experiences mimic Salinger's, and they stand in stark contrast to Holden's naivety and immaturity.

Though there's a clear gap between Holden's understanding of the world and the deeper awareness apparent between the lines of the novel, it's worth remembering that the three days described in *The Catcher in the Rye* are the darkest in Holden's short life. The few clues Salinger gives us about his future are optimistic – he is going back to school, and though he is immature now, his reactions to other people, and other people's advice, have shown that he is capable of empathising with others and absorbing the ideas he needs to grow and succeed as an adult. Perhaps the most optimistic thing of all is the fact that Holden is telling his own story so eloquently only a few months after the incidents described.

By telling his story Holden is fulfilling the prophecy Mr Antolini makes when he tells Holden people might one day be able to learn from him. Mr Antolini's carefully worded advice might well be a personal message from an author who's seen the worst of the world to a new generation of readers — and it may also be the best place to end this guide:

> *Among other things, you'll find that you're not the first person who was ever confused and frightened and even sickened by human behaviour ... Many, many men have been just as troubled morally and spiritually as you are right now. Happily, some of them kept records of their troubles. You'll learn from them – if you want to. Just as someday, if you have something to offer, someone will learn something from you. It's a beautiful reciprocal arrangement. And it isn't education. It's poetry.*

A SHORT CHRONOLOGY

1919 J.D. Salinger is born in Manhattan

1936 Enrols at New York University, before dropping out a year later

1938 Second World War breaks out

1942 Salinger is drafted into the US Army where he serves as an interrogator

1944 On D-Day, Salinger arrives on Utah Beach to participate in the invasion of Normandy

1948 "A Perfect Day for Bananafish" is published in the *New Yorker*

1949 *My Foolish Heart*, a film adaptation of Salinger's story "Uncle Wiggily in Connecticut," is released

1951 The Catcher in the Rye is published

1953 *Nine Stories*

1961 *Franny and Zooey*

1963 *Raise High the Roof Beam, Carpenters and Seymour: An Introduction*

2009 January 27 Salinger dies in Cornish, New Hampton

FURTHER READING

Useful works by J. D. Salinger
Salinger, J.D., "Interview with an Author" Interview, Shirley Blaney, Twin State Telescope

Salinger, J.D., Letter to a Mr. Herbert, 1956

Useful works for comparison by other authors
Burns, Robert, "Comin Thro' the Rye," *The Complete Work of Robert Burns*, Lansing, University of Michigan Press, 2006

Kerouac, Jack, *On The Road,* New York, Viking Press, 1957

Pierre, DBC, *Vernon God Little,* London, Canongate, 2002

Rakoff, Joanna, *My Salinger Year*, Bloomsbury Circus, 2014

Twain, Mark, *Adventures of Huckleberry Finn*, New York, Chatto & Windus, 1884

Useful Articles
Gopnick, Adam, "J.D. Salinger," The New Yorker

Kelly, Maura, "Must Every New Coming-of-age Novel be 'the Next Catcher in the Rye'?" The Atlantic

Lodge, David, "The Pre-Postmodernist," The New York Times

Malcolm, Janet, "Justice to JD Salinger," New York Review of Books

Menand, Louis, "Holden at Fifty," The New Yorker
Mills, Nancy, "Holden Caulfield's Many Pretenders," San Francisco Chronicle

Rohrer, Fiona, "Why Does Salinger's Catcher in the Rye Still Resonate?" BBC News Magazine

Rosenbaum, Ron, "He's Not Holden," Slate

Slawenski, Kenneth, "Holden Caulfield's Goddam War," Vanity Fair

Yardley, Jonathan, "J.D. Salinger's Holden Caulfield, Aging Gracelessly," The Washington Post

Useful Criticism
Alsen, Eberhard, *A Reader's Guide to J.D. Salinger,* Westport, Greenwood, 2002

Bloom, Harold (Ed.), *Modern Critical Interpretations: The Catcher in the Rye*, Chelsea House Publishers, Philadelphia, 2000

Dickstein, Morris, *Leopards in the Temple: The Transformation of American Fiction; 1945-1970,* Cambridge, Harvard University Press, 2002

Fiedler, Leslie A, *Love and Death in the American Novel,* Champaign, Dalkey Archive Press, 1960

French, Warren, *JD Salinger, Revisited,* Boston, Twayne, 1988
Hamilton, Ian, *In Search of J.D. Salinger*, London, Faber &

Faber, 1988

Heiserman, Arthur and James E. Miller Jr. "J. D. Salinger: Some Crazy Cliff'," Western Humanities Review, Spring 1956

Miller, Edwin Haviland, "Mourning Allie Caulfield," in *J. D. Salinger's The Catcher in the Rye*, ed. Harold Bloom, New York City, Bloom's Literary Criticism, 2007

Mueller, Bruce F. and Will Hochman, *Critical Companion to J. D. Salinger: A Literary Reference to his Life and Work*, New York City, Facts on File, 2010

Rosen, Gerald, "A Retrospective Look at The Catcher in the Rye," American Quarterly, Winter 1977

Strauch, Carl F., "Kings in the Back Row: Meaning through Structure" Wisconsin Studies in Contemporary Literature, Vol. 2, No.1, Winter 1961

Useful Reviews
Burger, Nash K., "Books of the Times," The New York Times, July 1951

Hughes, Riley, "New Novels," Catholic World, November 1951

Steiner, George, "The Salinger Industry," The Nation, November 14, 1959

Way, Brian, "Franny and Zooey" and J. D. Salinger', New Left Review, May/June 1962

Notes

First published in 2016 by
Connell Guides
Artist House
35 Little Russell Street
London WC1A 2HH

10 9 8 7 6 5 4 3 2 1

Picture credits:
p.23 © Moviestore / REX / Shutterstock
p.39 © KPA / Zooma / REX / Shutterstock

A CIP catalogue record for this book is available from the British Library.
ISBN 978-1-911187-04-2

Design © Nathan Burton
Written by Luke Neima
Editing by Jolyon Connell

Assistant Editors & typeset by:
Paul Woodward & Holly Bruce

www.connellguides.com

Printed and bound by CPI Group (UK) Ltd, Croydon, CR0 4YY